To
Lynne.
Hope to see you at the
Celery Farm.

J W

In the Presence of Nature

The Celery Farm Natural Area
Allendale, New Jersey

"The sun illuminates only the eye of the man, but shines into the eye and the heart of the child. The lover of nature is he whose inward and outward senses are still truly adjusted to each other; who has retained the spirit of infancy even into the era of manhood. . . . In the presence of nature, a wild delight runs through the man, in spite of real sorrows."

— from the essay "Nature," by Ralph Waldo Emerson (1836)

Douglas Goodell provided additional photography, technical expertise, and inestimable help. Patrick Sparkman provided additional photography.

The support of the Fyke Nature Association and the New Jersey Conservation Foundation has been crucial to both the Celery Farm and to this book. For more information, contact NJCF at www.njconservation.org and Fyke at www.fykenature.org.

For Adrienne and Patty

Facing page: A Clouded Sulphur Butterfly nectaring on a blanketflower

In the Presence of Nature

The Celery Farm Natural Area
Allendale, New Jersey

Photography by Jerry Barrack   Text by Jim Wright

Camino Books, Inc. • Philadelphia

Printed in China

1 2 3 4 5 06 05 04 03

Library of Congress Cataloging-in-Publication Data

Barrack, Jerry.
    In the presence of nature : the Celery Farm Natural Area / photography
by Jerry Barrack ; text by Jim Wright.
        p. cm.
    ISBN 0–940159–75–9 (hardcover : alk. paper)
 1. Natural history—New Jersey—Allendale—Pictorial works. 2. Celery
Farm Natural Area (Allendale, N.J.)—Pictorial works. I. Wright, Jim.
II. Title.
    QH105.N5 B36 2002
    508.749'21—dc21

                                                    2002001804

Cover and interior design: Amy Blake

Introduction by Stiles Thomas adapted from his article in *New Jersey Audubon*, Winter 1995–96

Bird and nature quotations were excerpted from several sources, including *An Exhilaration of Wings*, edited by Jen Hill (Penguin Books); *The Great House of Birds*, edited by John Hay (Sierra Club Books); *Nature's Places*, by Rod Planck and Bert C. Ebbers (Hawk-Owl Publishing); and the writings of John Burroughs and Henry David Thoreau

Excerpt from *Ospreys*, by Alan J. Poole, reprinted with permission of Cambridge University Press

Excerpt on winter at the Celery Farm, written by Christopher DeVinck, from *Only the Heart Knows How to Find Them* (Viking Press)

Excerpt on pond hockey at the Celery Farm, by Charles McGrath, first published in *Outside* magazine, 1997

This book is available at a special discount on bulk purchases for promotional, business, and educational use. For information write to:

Publisher
Camino Books, Inc.
P.O. Box 59026
Philadelphia, PA 19102

www.caminobooks.com

Contents

The late Edward FitzPatrick

Stiles Thomas

This book is dedicated to two great Americans, whose

vision saved a singular patch of land, water, and sky.

Foreword

By David Allen Sibley

Humans have had an impact on virtually every inch of North America, and perhaps nowhere more than in northeastern New Jersey, where centuries of industry, agriculture, and human settlement have erased most of the natural landscape.

The days of wilderness exploration in this country are gone. We are no longer struggling to tame the natural world, but coaxing along little patches of it in sanctuaries and preserves the way a gardener tends a garden. Like gardens, these patches of natural habitat are literally sanctuaries, for people as well as for wildlife.

Places like the Celery Farm provide the space to stretch out, relax, and experience the beauty of nature. Nothing can replace the peace and rejuvenation that we feel when walking in the still air of early morning, or studying the colors of the fall leaves, listening to the birds' songs, or seeing unexpectedly a great blue heron or an osprey.

It is a testament to nature that the Celery Farm provides such a rich and diverse natural community. It is amazing that such things as mink and kingfishers exist, thrive, and live their normal lives in a 107-acre sanctuary surrounded by urban sprawl. It is amazing that all of the exquisite photographs in this book were taken on those 107 acres.

Most of all, this book is a testament to the vision of the people who have worked to preserve the land. It doesn't take a lot of space, or a lot of money, just people who care. The Celery Farm, once an undistinguished little wetland among farms or forest, is now a very distinguished sanctuary, a gem among sprawl. It is a sign of hope for the future that this place has been preserved, and one can hope that it, and this book, will inspire other similar sanctuaries.

Wouldn't it be great if every town had a Celery Farm?

"A lake is the landscape's most beautiful and expressive feature. It is the earth's eye; looking into which the beholder measures the depth of his own nature."

— Henry David Thoreau, Walden *(1854)*

Introduction

By Stiles Thomas, Marsh Warden

If you promise not to tell anyone, I'll tell you about a delightful place to watch birds, take a walk through woods and wetlands, or just commune with nature. It's called the Celery Farm, and it's in northeastern New Jersey not all that far from Manhattan.

We've all heard the horror tales about national parks being trampled by hordes of people, and you wouldn't want to be responsible should this happen to this hundred-and-seven-acre refuge, would you? So remember, this is just between us. If you encounter someone on the trail, don't let on that I was the one to divulge this well-kept secret.

Every photograph in this book was taken at the Celery Farm. Although more than 230 species of birds have been found in the refuge, don't expect to see more than a fraction of that number in an hour's walk. After all, these images were accumulated over thousands of hours at all times of day, and all times of year, for more than a decade. This book is a sort of "Celery Farm Greatest Hits" album.

In 1981 the borough of Allendale acquired a sixty-acre parcel of black-earth wetlands. Since then, the rest was obtained from neighboring property owners. Acquisition of the Celery Farm was made possible by the New Jersey Conservation Foundation. The NJCF bought the property and held it until the town could buy it with the help of funds from New Jersey's Green Acres Program.

Mayor Edward FitzPatrick was instrumental in bringing this all about. When the title passed from the NJCF to the town, he authorized the Fyke Nature Association to turn the land into a nature preserve. He also appointed me marsh warden. Since then, the group has constructed observation platforms, bridges, and paths. It has also engaged in several other projects — from a wood-duck nesting-box program to a revolutionary tree-swallow nesting experiment.

The trails at the Celery Farm are maintained by Mike Limatola and other dedicated members of Fyke. The borough of Allendale has no appropriation for the Farm. Everything is done by volunteers — with the borough's Department of Public Works, under the direction of George Higbie, helping with the heavy challenges.

Several people who have visited the Farm say it reminds them at times of a footpath through the English countryside. See if you don't feel the same when you walk the trail along the Allendale Brook. But don't forget, mum's the word.

Near the Allendale Brook

Out of the mist

Chapter 1

Beginnings

"Those who contemplate the beauty of the Earth find reserves of strength that will endure as long as life lasts. There is symbolic as well as actual beauty in the migration of birds, the ebb and flow of tides, the folded bud ready for spring. There is something infinitely healing in the repeated refrains of nature — the assurance that dawn comes after the night and spring after the winter."

— *Rachel Carson,* The Sense of Wonder *(1965)*

It's early October, just before dawn, with only a breeze across the water to disturb the stillness. As the sun peers over the horizon, the marsh springs to life.

On the mist-shrouded lake, Canada geese honk their discordant reveille and flap past a great blue heron who stands vigil in the shallows. Soon, legions of grackles and starlings cackle like anxious recruits. Nearby, platoons of egrets and mallards and wood ducks bide their time.

Then, as if on cue, the Celery Farm avian air corps mobilizes. The activity at Newark International Airport, twenty-five miles to the south, can't compare. This lake, these marshes, will see as many departures in the next few moments as the runways of Newark handle in a week.

First, thousands upon thousands of the smaller birds depart, peppering the sunrise. Next come the squadrons of obstreperous geese. Then the ducks. Amid the commotion, a stately great egret glides from his willow perch and settles into his spot along the shore: The early bird catches the carp.

Listen closer and you'll realize that the relentless reach of mankind is not far off. Just to the east, cars and sport utility vehicles thrum along the six-lane commuter conveyor known as Route 17. To the west, a passenger train hoots a wakeup call as it clatters into the Allendale station. High above, a nameless jetliner presses onward.

The miracle of all this is twofold.

It is a wonder that this fragile haven can thrive in the New York metropolitan region, the nation's most densely populated.

It is a wonder that this place, the Celery Farm Natural Area, exists at all.

Birds pepper the early-morning sky

Great Blue Heron with large-mouth bass

Chapter 2

The fishermen

"A fishing heron is the very model of patience, standing motionless in the shallows, waiting for that critical fraction of a second in which to lunge and transfix its prey with that formidable javelin of a bill."

— *Dennis Puleston,* A Nature Journal *(1992)*

The signs at the entrances to the Celery Farm proclaim no fishing, but that's not quite so. Humans cannot fish here, but for several species of birds and a mammal or two, Lake Appert and its two small ponds might as well be the self-serve fish department at the local grocery.

Great blue herons, green herons, black-crowned night herons, double-crested cormorants, great egrets, and the dynamic little belted kingfisher all use their bills to snag the carp, sunnies, and other fish.

Great Egret catching a sunfish

Belted Kingfisher

"A feathered [Isaak] Walton who is a stickler for his fishing rights."

— *T. Gilbert Pearson,*
Birds of America *(1917)*

Great Blue Heron

"None of them are beautiful on close inspection, but most are graceful in their movements when walking, and many exceedingly so when on the wing. It is eminently true of them that distance lends enchantment to the view, and the less said about the merits of their singing, the better."

> *— Charles C. Abbott,*
> A Naturalist's Rambles About Home
> *(1885)*

Mink at water's edge

These birds are the easiest to spot from the viewing platforms on the lake's southern and eastern rim. And they can be the most fun to watch as they glide above the water, stalk their prey at water's edge, or, in the case of the cormorant, dive under water.

The resident mink may be the best fish-grabber of all. It's tough to say because he's rarely seen. The best time to see him is in early May, when the weather is warming and the trees have yet to sport their new spring wardrobes. He might lurk on the peninsula near the main entrance, plunging into the water and emerging moments later with a huge catfish in his mouth. Once he's sure it's dead, he'll drag it into a well-hidden burrow. People aren't the only ones who prefer to eat indoors.

Green Heron

Which is the Snowy Egret, and which is the Little Blue Heron? You decide.

"Like other white herons, this exquisite little egret, although once abundant, has been practically exterminated by persistent hunting for its plumes."
— *Arthur H. Howell,* Birds of Arkansas *(1911)*

For showmanship, the osprey is tops. The large fish hawk begins her hunt by circling Lake Appert. When she spies a fish — most often a bright-orange carp — she follows it from aloft. Alan J. Poole, in his book, *Ospreys,* describes the process precisely: " . . . fishing ospreys fly slowly, sometimes circling back on themselves and often pulling up briefly to hover before moving on again, apparently stalking their prey. . . .

"The dive itself is spectacular, a quick release of tension built up during the preceding minutes. A diving osprey tucks back its wings and abandons itself to the pull of gravity, usually falling steeply but maneuvering subtly with its wing and tail all the while, to keep on track toward its target. . . .

Osprey in flight

Osprey hits the water

Osprey begins her takeoff

"Try landing a fish 15 to 30 percent of your own weight with your bare hands and you will begin to appreciate the problem of an osprey lifting its struggling prey from the water. Even if the bird's talons strike deep, most fish are tough, die slowly, and struggle violently. To combat this, ospreys often rest briefly on the water after diving, probably securing their prey, and then reach high with long, fast, almost horizontal wing strokes that start well above the tail and sweep down and forward of the head to eye level. The birds seem to gain much of their lift with the outer tips of their wings, taking off slowly like helicopters with heavy payloads. Once airborne, an osprey usually rearranges its prey, one foot ahead of the other, so the fish's head points forward and its body is tucked close to the bird. This cuts wind resistance and speeds flight back to nest or perch."

Osprey with carp

Chapter 3

A walk around the refuge

"The witness of the eye alone would persuade us that nature had achieved the whole result."

—Frederick Law Olmsted on parks and wetlands

The man who planned Manhattan's Central Park and Boston's Fenway, Frederick Law Olmsted, knew a thing or two about incorporating marshes into his designs — out of pure necessity. By the time town fathers understood that open space was crucial to their cities' health, the remaining land was usually swamp.

Canada Geese take a hike

Similar circumstances explain the Celery Farm Natural Area. The property has always been too swampy to build much on. The refuge, established on bog-like celery fields more than two decades ago, looks to the casual observer that it has always been thus: a naturally formed collection of ponds and marshes with ancient paths. In fact, it took a lot of work — primarily by volunteers — to develop those trails and shape the old farmland into a wildlife sanctuary. If one of America's major environmental challenges of the last century was to save dwindling open space, then the challenge for this century could well be to restore these lands to a more pristine state. The Celery Farm can help show the way.

The biggest expanse of water is Lake Appert, the size of a few football fields. Circling the lake is a flat path, a country mile long. Two large observation platforms, a smaller stand, and benches provide places for people to sit and watch the wildlife. Side trails lead to two smaller ponds, Heron Pond to the east and Phair's Pond to the north.

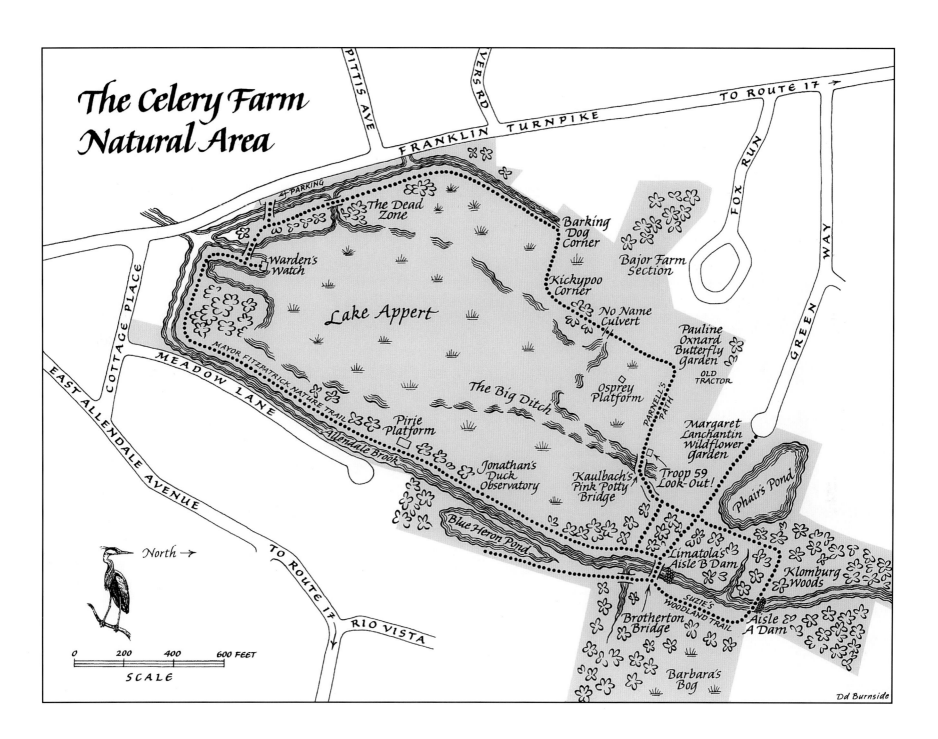

The Celery Farm Natural Area

PITTIS AVE

VERS RD

FRANKLIN TURNPIKE

TO ROUTE 17 →

FOX RUN

GREEN WAY

PARKING

The Dead Zone

Barking Dog Corner

Warden's Watch

Bajor Farm Section

Kickypoo Corner

No Name Culvert

Lake Appert

Pauline Oxnard Butterfly Garden

OLD TRACTOR

COTTAGE PLACE

MEADOW LANE

MAYOR FITZPATRICK NATURE TRAIL

The Big Ditch

Osprey Platform

PARNELL'S PATH

Margaret Lanchantin Wildflower Garden

Pirie Platform

Allendale Brook

EAST ALLENDALE AVENUE

Jonathan's Duck Observatory

Kaulbach's Pink Potty Bridge

Troop 59 Look-Out!

Phair's Pond

Blue Heron Pond

Limatola's Aisle B Dam

Klomburg Woods

North →

TO ROUTE 17

RIO VISTA

Brotherton Bridge

SUZIE'S WOODLAND TRAIL

Aisle A Dam

Barbara's Bog

0   200   400   600 FEET
SCALE

Dd Burnside

33

Male Ring-necked Pheasant

What you'll see depends on when you go.

In winter, the refuge is sleeping, recharging its batteries. On a cold windless morning, with the ground crunching underneath, a visit to the Celery Farm resembles walking through a sepia black-and-white photograph.

Late April and early May offer the best times for viewing nature. The weather is warming, the migrating birds are arriving in force, and, since most trees don't have their leaves yet, the wildlife is easier to spot. This is when such rare sights as a mink, a red fox, a prothonotary warbler, and a cerulean warbler have appeared.

Summer is the season of herons, egrets, and swallows. The flowers and plants are at full throttle, and so are the frogs and turtles.

In autumn, the attractions are the changing foliage and the arrivals of the migratory birds, including ducks of every feather.

For most, a walk around the refuge begins in a small parking lot off Franklin Turnpike, a half-mile from the bustle of Route 17. You needn't bring

Young Ring-necked Pheasant

anything special, although good binoculars and comfortable walking shoes are advised. Bug repellant is recommended in summer. Nature guidebooks can come in handy to identify the various birds, bugs, trees, and plants.

The first stop is a small bulletin board by the entrance. Under the writing surface is a loose-leaf notebook that features a map of the refuge's walking paths as well as birders' notes on species seen in recent days and where they were spotted. In the more than two decades that the natural area has been in existence, birders have sighted some 230 species, from the too-common Canada goose to the exotic purple gallinule and red-necked phalarope. Any time of year, you will likely see mallards, crows, and perhaps a pheasant. Fifty-five species breed here.

The bulletin board lists a few rules: Stay on the paths, don't pick the wildflowers, and beware of poison ivy.

If you bring a dog, bring a pooper scooper and a leash. Dogs can attack pheasants, snipes, and other creatures who take refuge here. That's why an Allendale ordinance calls for a hundred-dollar fine for people who don't keep their dogs leashed at the Farm.

A few steps across a short wooden bridge and you're in the refuge (see map, page 33). If you head counterclockwise — the preferred route in the morning because the sun won't get in your eyes as much — you'll walk through a knotweed forest. These bamboo-like plants grow up to eight feet tall in summer. Cross another bridge, and fifteen yards to your left will be a viewing platform called the Warden's Watch. Many people come to the refuge just to sit on the platform. In the summer twilight, you can study egrets roosting in the trees or watch great blue herons stalk one last fish before bedtime.

If you feel up to a challenge, try matching your birding skills against the local eagle eyes, who spend an "hour on the tower" every Sunday morning August through October. They identify an average of thirty species during each sixty-minute go-'round.

Continuing on the path, you'll soon pass a small secluded pond where an occasional duck or snapping turtle lingers, then it's around a bend and onto the portion of the path that reminds so many of an English country lane. The Allendale Brook is to your right. Where the path nears the shoreline, the splash of frogs may precede your steps. Halfway down the east side of the lake, on your left, is another observation deck, the Pirie Platform. Here you might get great views of wading birds and a belted kingfisher or two.

A few years back, the marsh warden closed the main path near the Pirie Platform for a month to protect a wintering roost of five long-eared owls, a threatened species. The Celery Farm is one of those rare places in suburbia where nature comes first.

Keep heading counterclockwise and you'll eventually cross two more small bridges, which mark the halfway point. A Virginia rail likes to hang out here in late winter. Just past the

Rainy days and white-throats

"A day of silver rain, pouring down straight and tumultuously on the roofs, on the trees; silver rain like a flight of javelins blown down from the sky. And the white-throat singing, perhaps for the last time before this little winter resident takes flight. . . . "

— *Donald Culross Peattie,*

An Almanac for Moderns *(1935)*

Deer in the Big Ditch

Chipmunk

Bullfrog

Painted Turtle

Rabbit

"And this, our life, exempt from public haunt, finds tongues in trees, books

in the running brooks, sermons in stones, and good in everything."

— William Shakespeare

THE
PAULINE OXNARD
BUTTERFLY GARDEN

"I go to nature to be soothed and healed, and to have my senses put in order."

— *John Burroughs*

bridges is a platform called the Troop 59 Look-Out. Next comes a phragmites forest. When you reach the clearing, you'll see a broken-down tractor, a remnant of an age when the lake was drained and the place was a working farm. Celery farms and naturalists go back a long way. One of the great nature writers of the nineteenth century, John Burroughs, lived next to a celery bog sixty miles due north.

The old tractor is a Cletrac — short for the Cleveland Tractor Company. It was built in 1934. The machine is a favorite for young children to climb upon. Cletracs have an international following among farm-equipment buffs. Some claim that with enough parts and patience they could get the old gal running again. At the Celery Farm, hope springs eternal.

A few steps further is the Pauline Oxnard Butterfly Garden, created in memory of a friend of the refuge. There's a small bench for rest and contemplation. It's also a popular hangout of the oft-elusive pheasants.

Keep going and you'll pass wetlands on both sides. As summer progresses, you'll see a lot of waist-high plants with orange buds. These plants go by a variety of quaint names — jewelweed, touch-me-nots, poppers. The buds are lovely, and if you get stung by a bug or scratched by a thorn, you're permitted to break the refuge's rules and pick a jewelweed stem in order to rub its soothing natural salve on your skin. In late September, you'll see why the plant is called a popper or a touch-me-not. Put your fingers to one of the small green pods and it will gently explode.

A few more turns, and you're back at the main entrance. Don't forget to note in the loose-leaf book any unusual birds or animals you saw, and where you saw them.

Great Spangled Fritillary

Cabbage White Butterfly

Clear-winged Hummingbird Moth

Eastern Tiger Swallowtail

Jewelweed

"Like Japanese haiku poetry, sometimes more is less . . . in nature,

beauty or meaning need not be on a large scale."

—*Jim Brandenburg,* Chased by the Light *(1998)*

Male Northern Shoveler

Common Snipe

Male Ring-necked Pheasant preening

Female Mute Swan with cygnet

"Hope is a thing with feathers." — Emily Dickinson

Chapter 4

In the swim

"The duck was all jewels combined, showing different lusters as turned on the unrippled element in various lights, now brilliant glossy green, now dusky violet, now a rich bronze, now the reflections that sleep in the ruby's grain."

— *Henry David Thoreau,* Journal *(1855)*

If you frequent the Celery Farm in the spring or autumn, you'll appreciate the importance of wetlands to water fowl and other migratory birds, who can fly thousands of miles in the course of their travels.

During October the refuge becomes a bed and breakfast for ducks.

Female Wood Duck

Young Wood Ducks

What many people call pond scum is more affectionately known as duckweed. It may not be the breakfast of champions, but it is the meal of choice for mallards and mergansers.

Wood ducks reside in the refuge much of the year. Each spring, the female wood ducks make their nests in the wooden boxes near the shore of Lake Appert, then raise their young on the lake. So often, nature's most beautiful creatures are also the most fragile. A wood duck has as many as nine ducklings at a time because they are so vulnerable to predators, especially the snapping turtles who patrol the lake like U-boats.

The mute swans at Lake Appert can be as ephemeral as sun showers. You may see them daily for weeks, then not again for years. This is one of the refuge's many lessons: Few things in life are certain. Savor them while you can.

Double-crested Cormorant

Male Hooded Merganser

Male Hooded Merganser

Female Green-winged Teal

Pied-billed Grebe

Male Ruddy Duck

Female Hooded Merganser

Male Wood Duck

"It was a splendid bird, a perfect floating gem, and [my companion], who had never seen the like, was greatly surprised, not knowing that so splendid a bird was found in this part of the world."

—*Henry David Thoreau,* Journal *(1845)*

The farm in its heyday

"And the world cannot be discovered by a journey of miles, no matter how long, but only by a spiritual journey, a journey of one inch, very arduous and humbling and joyful, by which we arrive at the ground at our feet, and learn to be at home."

— Wendell Berry, The Unforeseen Wilderness *(1971)*

Chapter 5

A sense of place

"Once in his life, a man ought to concentrate his mind on the remembered earth. He ought to give himself up to a particular landscape in his experience; to look at it from as many angles as he can, to wander upon it, to dwell upon it."

— *N. Scott Momaday,* The Way to Rainy Mountain *(1969)*

A few miles south of the Ramapo Mountains, on the Piedmont Plain, sits Lake Appert and the heart of the Celery Farm Natural Area.

In a process that took eons, this shallow body of water has come full circle, from lake to bog to farm to lake. Many millennia ago, glaciers crept across North America, carving out valleys and basins. When the ice melted, the water transported huge quantities of sand and gravel into the lower-lying areas.

Along the highlands to the west of the Hudson River, a small lake formed in one of those depressions, and vegetation took root. As the plants decomposed, swampland encroached on

Henry J. Appert, founder of the Celery Farm

the open water. The Wolf Clan of the Lenni Lenape Indians were among the first humans to encounter the lake, a few thousand years ago. If one can judge from the arrowheads and primitive tools found in the area, the shallow lake and the Allendale Brook that runs through it provided a fertile hunting ground.

The 1600s brought the Europeans, the eventual colonization of the area, and the demise of the Lenni Lenapes. By the time of the Revolutionary War, the lake had become a bog packed with thick black peat. Maps back then called the area "Wolf Swamp."

In the mid-nineteenth century came the settlers. They cleared the forests for farmland, and peat became increasingly popular as a fuel. An enterprising developer got the idea of excavating and selling the sod from Wolf Swamp. Newspaper clippings from 1866 and 1884 tell the story of the enterprise's rise and fall:

"The work of developing these valuable resources was begun in Allendale, where J. J. Zabriskie of Ho-Ho-Kus has purchased a peat meadow which we judge to be about a mile in length and varying from a quarter to a half in breadth. A large force of hands was immediately set to work, and are now engaged in draining the grounds. It is intended to lower the main ditch running through it about two feet, which will drain the bog about 12 feet down, to which depth the deposit is known to extend. Cost of work, building machinery &c necessary to commence the manufacture it is estimated will be about $10,000."

— *The Weekly Press* (Paterson), August 9, 1866

"The old building in the middle of the big meadows at Allendale is a relic of the days when John J. Zabriskie, of Ho-Ho-Kus, thought there were millions in peat."

—*Paterson Weekly Guardian*, April 18, 1884

Zabriskie's lack of success wasn't for a lack of trying. He even installed a narrow-gauge rail track for several hundred feet along what is now the eastern edge of the natural area. Laborers cut the moist sod into blocks, stacked them in the sun to dry, then loaded them onto flat-bed rail cars. Horses pulled the cars to a loading area, where the peat was placed in wagons at Franklin Turnpike for its trip to market. By the time Zabriskie finished, he had created a huge mucky gulch.

As the region's population swelled, farms gave way to houses, but the oft-flooded swampland lay abandoned by all but birds and animals — and the outdoorsmen who pursued them. Europeans had been converting stripped peat bogs into farmlands for centuries. A Swiss immigrant named Henry J. Appert and his wife Ella Finn Appert saw

Men in the field

Celery Farm truck

what remained of Wolf Swamp and decided to drain it and convert it into fields. They bought the property in 1888, and — as the Apperts' daughter Ella wrote in an article for the Allendale Historical Society — "it took a couple of years to clear the land and to prepare, throughout, a complete vein of drainage."

First they grew onions. Then celery.

Although the business was called the Allendale Produce Gardens and it grew all sorts of crops, including pumpkins, it became known as Apperts' Farm or simply "the Celery Farm." The Apperts' son Arthur took over the farm in 1915 and, despite a huge fire in 1935 that destroyed four farm buildings, the business flourished. Wrote Ms. Appert: "Loads of produce were

"King Arthur" Appert

conveyed by motor truck and in refrigerated railroad cars to the wholesale markets in New York City, Boston, Paterson, and to the Campbell Soup factory. The Celery was branded and became famed as the Triple A and King Arthur brands."

Ms. Appert's niece, Mary Appert Schneider, says her uncle Arthur improved the celery crop by growing spinach and plowing it into the fields each fall. She says her brother Edward used to build crates at a half-penny per crate — and eventually made enough crates to pay for his first car.

In 1943, Arthur Appert retired and sold the enterprise to McBride, Inc., owned by Paterson developer J. Nevins McBride. By several accounts, working at the farm was tough labor. One former hand, Don Wallworth, recalls working there as a Ramsey teenager in the mid-1940s. He says he always had a sure but difficult way to make a little cash: "Show up early in the morning at the Allendale Celery Farm."

He could earn money two ways: building celery crates or working in the field. The prize job — which he never got — was making the crates. Instead, he says, he joined many Polish immigrants and "ended up with the intolerable job spent on your hands and knees, weeding. The black wet earth, turned to mud, stuck to everything. In no time your clothes were covered, your knees matted in mire clinging in layers. The back aches came early, and standing up to stretch too often brought attention from field foremen that patrolled along the rows. To avoid time spent going to the water spout in the unbearable heat, water was brought to you, and none too often."

Another young worker, Paul Shannon, was luckier. He recalls that in the late 1940s, he helped build the crates to ship the celery nationwide. He was barely ten years old.

"I would ride my bicycle early in the morning from Waldwick, and then pound nails all day into wood slats that we placed into a form," he says. "When the form was finished, we had a box that the celery was packed into, moved to a huge wash house, placed on trucks, and shipped away. To this day, I can still smell the overwhelming aroma of celery as it sat in that wash house.

"As a child of the Depression, I was happy to be able to work anywhere and make a few dollars to buy clothes, a bike, or whatever. I still have a scar on my left arm where I put my hand into a barrel of nails, and a nail from the barrel lid tore into my arm.

"Whenever I go back East and drive by the 'jungle' that used to be the farm, I remember those wonderful days of youth, when life was real simple — it was survival."

The farm struggled as well. For one thing, the land tended to flood, despite all the

Aerial view, mid-1950s

The fish hatchery

drainage ditches and a pump house that had been installed to extract the excess water. A major flood in 1945 destroyed the farm's entire crop.

The farm went out of business by the mid-1950s. McBride sold several acres east of the Allendale Brook to a hatchery and aquarium supply business. Some say the orange carp that dart around Lake Appert are descendants of refugees from the hatchery.

Local naturalist Stiles Thomas had always had it in his head that the land should be preserved as open space. He had hunted on the farm's fringes as a boy, and he knew better than most the variety of wildlife that wetlands attract. In 1956, when McBride first offered the land for sale, Thomas wrote to the U.S. Fish and Wildlife Service and proposed that the agency "secure the land as a preserve." Thomas conceded that the area was small compared with most sanctuaries that the agency ran but added ruefully: "Wet lands are hard to find nowadays."

A bureaucrat wrote back that the price "is greatly in excess of any figure previously paid for waterfowl lands, and it is unlikely that such a proposal would be given favorable consideration." It was one of many rejections that Thomas would get in his quest to save the marshes over the next quarter century.

In the 1970s, the land was still for sale, and people talked of making it into a golf course. At that point, Thomas found an ally in another far-sighted Allendale resident — its mayor, Edward FitzPatrick. After repeated nudges, FitzPatrick arrived at Thomas' insurance office one day and said a dozen words that changed everything: "So, what do we have to do to save the Celery Farm?"

Once Mayor FitzPatrick became committed to saving the farm, things slowly fell into place. One of

J. Nevins McBride's sons, Peter, was in charge of developing the property, and he was increasingly frustrated that he spent so much of his time trying to keep the land dry. He wanted to sell — for the right price.

Enter the New Jersey Conservation Foundation (NJCF). Since its founding in 1960, the foundation's mission has been to preserve environmentally valuable land in the public interest. The foundation works with all levels of government to choose property worth saving, negotiate with the owners, then come up with the funding to buy and hold the land until public officials can raise enough money.

Over the years, the foundation has helped save 77,000 acres in New Jersey — from the Walt Whitman House in Camden to the Wallkill National Wildlife Refuge in a northern corner of the state.

Cletrac tractor

For the NJCF, the Celery Farm was a natural. Says David Moore, the executive director at the time: "We took one look and knew this was a place worth saving. Here, in the middle of suburbia, were these marvelous wetlands, filled with herons and egrets and all sorts of creatures."

Thomas and his allies made a strong case for keeping the land undeveloped, citing its value as a place where flood waters from the Upper Saddle River and Ramsey watersheds could collect and reduce flooding downstream. They also re-ported that nearly 200 bird species, including such endangered species as the peregrine falcon and bald eagle, had been seen at the Celery Farm.

"Vegetation in a wetland such as this helps create the richest of wildlife habitats," they wrote in *The Celery Farm: Its Natural History*. "Here is ample food and shelter for insects, aquatic life, animals and birds; and this, in turn, affords an ideal situation for an outdoor laboratory and a place where unspoiled nature can be an unforgettable experience."

Peter McBride met with Moore and Darryl Caputo of the NJCF, and they eventually struck a deal: $170,000 for sixty mostly swampy acres. Said Peter McBride at the time, "We're in the real estate business and, ideally, we would have liked to develop part of the Celery Farm. But Darryl did the legwork and put together a package that we're reasonably happy with, and it's good for the town."

Through New Jersey's Green Acres program, Allendale received enough money in matching grants to take possession of the property. In 1981, it became the first town in America to purchase wetlands and save them as open space.

As Mayor FitzPatrick told *The New York Times:* "The idea is not to build anything on it. We're not trying to keep people out, and accessibility is pretty good. But this is not a park, it's a natural area."

Thomas and a local group of bird-watchers and conservationists, the Fyke Nature Association, volunteered to improve and maintain the land. They began all sorts of projects, from restoring habitat to building trails around the lake.

The only person who seemed irked by it all was J. Nevins McBride, who complained in a local newspaper that he had intended that the property remain drained of water and left in a condition that would permit athletics: "We were upset to see it revert to a bird sanctuary, although it is pleasant to walk through it in a very limited fashion."

Indeed, humans at the refuge have come under tighter controls over the years so that it can fulfill its mission as a wildlife refuge. Boating was prohibited because it disrupted birds, particularly during nesting. Fishing was banned as well because it was tantamount to hunting in a nature preserve, and because birds kept getting entangled in discarded nylon-filament fishing line. The town has tended to look the other way in regard to the generations-old tradition of ice-skating there. Lake Appert has been home to many spirited pond-hockey games.

Meanwhile, as word continued to spread that Allendale was a great place to live and raise a family, Thomas kept campaigning to save as much of the adjacent woods and farmland as he could. Most of the available real estate, including the nearby Bajor Farm, was falling victim to bulldozers.

Each time a developer wanted to subdivide, Thomas worked to secure a chunk of land to add to the Celery Farm: Would a developer be interested in giving, say, several acres to the natural area in exchange for permission to build more housing per acre?

Often the answer was yes, but often that reply came after the developers had tried — legally or otherwise — to get their way. In other instances, success came in the form of zoning victories that kept developers from building or paving too close to what are the largest fresh-water wetlands left in Bergen County. And local property owners helped in at least one instance, donating three acres behind their home so the nature trail that circles most of the preserve could be completed.

Today the Celery Farm Natural Area has grown to more than 100 acres, surrounded mostly by houses, condominiums, and an industrial park. It won't be getting much bigger: Virtually no more nearby open land remains.

That makes the Celery Farm all the more treasured, both by the humans who "walk through it in a very limited fashion" and by the creatures who find sanctuary here.

The old Bajor barn in winter

Osprey in action

Chapter 6

Rare creatures and action shots

"Why, sometimes I've believed six impossible things before breakfast."

— *Lewis Carroll,* Through the Looking Glass *(1872)*

Walk around the main path at the Celery Farm enough, and sooner or later you'll see all sorts of extraordinary things — from star-nosed moles to wonderful warblers to a killer bullfrog.

One of the beauties of photography is that it can capture a sight as fleeting as the beat of a belted kingfisher's wing. On the following pages are pictures of sights seldom seen at the

Purple Gallinule

Celery Farm. Among the most memorable was a twelve-day visit by a rainbow-colored Southern bird, the purple gallinule, in August 2001.

Birders traveled hundreds of miles to the Celery Farm for a look at the elusive bird, which usually doesn't go much farther north than the Carolinas. A doctor in his surgical scrubs drove thirty miles between operations in hopes of adding the gallinule to his life list — the list of bird species he has seen. The gallinule, who appeared sporadically amid the loosestrife each day until midafternoon, was a first for serious birders who hadn't traveled much down South.

In May of that year, a pair of uncommon warblers, the cerulean and the prothonotary, made fleeting appearances (pages 78 and 79). Neither had been seen in the refuge in many years, and both were accommodating enough to perch in trees and bushes not far from the main entrance.

A few days later, a bullfrog grabbed the limelight by drowning a Canada gosling (page 85) in the stream near where the cerulean and prothonotary had sung. The bullfrog, too, seemed to pose for astonished onlookers. He managed to get his mouth around the young bird's head and pulled it underwater while the mother goose squawked furiously.

A red-necked phalarope and pine siskins made an appearance that year as well.

Red foxes live in the refuge, but you had better be near the two little bridges at the north end of the lake before dawn if you have hope of glimpsing one.

Long-eared Owl

Cerulean Warbler

Prothonotary Warbler

Great Egret gets too close to a Red-winged Blackbird's nest

Sharp-shinned Hawk

Broad-winged Hawk

Female Northern Harrier

Snakes, frogs, and painted turtles are familiar sights, if you remember to look down as often as you look up.

None of the snake species found here is poisonous, and the most aggressive creature is a Canada goose trying to protect its young. That made the bullfrog's cold-blooded slaying of a gosling that much more extraordinary.

Snapping turtles are the most blatant predators, attacking anything that moves in the water. Still, one summer morning it was startling to see a huge turtle devour a double-crested cormorant like a chainsaw going through pine (photo, page 84). Nature's food chain looks better in print than in person.

Northern Water Snake

Snapping Turtle devours a Double-crested Cormorant

Bullfrog drowns a gosling

Red Fox

Fox tracks

"How winter emphasizes the movements of wild life! The snow and

the cold are the white paper upon which the print is revealed."

—*John Burroughs,* Birds and Bees *(1887)*

Chapter 7

The art of seeing

"Look deep into nature, and then you will understand everything better."

— *Albert Einstein*

A hummingbird zipping past the loosestrife. A red fox vanishing into the thicket. Green herons nesting. A belted kingfisher catching a sunny. To see nature in its many incarnations, you don't have to travel far. You just need to find a natural place, visit it often, and learn to see with new eyes.

The Celery Farm is a great place to view nature because it contains marsh, field, forest, and open water, and the path around the lake brings you into contact with all four elements. But you'll notice soon that some people see a lot more than others. The difference has more to do with the power of their senses than the power of their binoculars.

Those whose birding skills lean toward the crow, the great egret, and the not-so-great Canada goose have a sense of wonder about people who can identify a song sparrow at the drop of a trill. The secret is simple. They've studied a lot and observed more — often since childhood. And they have cultivated a heightened awareness.

Study and observation can hone your nature skills. As with any other pastime, nature appreciation increases proportionately with one's knowledge of the subject. A rose by any other name may smell as sweet, but without a name it is simply a flower. Without a name, a kingfisher is just an enchanting little bird.

Over time, you can learn to identify most birds.

The question is, how do you see them — especially when the leaves are on the trees?

You need what John Burroughs called "sharp eyes" — the ability to see nature in ways others cannot. If, as Henry David Thoreau maintained, most people go through life half-asleep, then the best way to observe the Celery Farm — and life in general — is to be wide awake to the possibilities. A healthy curiosity, a dollop of patience, and an ability to cast aside personal concerns can enable you to learn to see all sorts of things.

A walk on the main path around the Celery Farm can take half an hour, or half a day. How much you get out of it depends on how much you invest. Some suggestions:

Go early. The early birder sees the most.

Go alone. Thoreau said he always walked by himself because he didn't have any walks to waste. Walking with others was too distracting. You can't hear a Carolina wren if you're talking.

Lincoln Sparrow

If you can't walk alone, go with an expert. Choose a companion who can identify birds by eye or ear, someone who can transmit the love of things natural, someone who knows where various birds are apt to be.

Or take a curious child. They see what adults miss — from spiders' webs to frogs to pond-shrouded turtles. They're usually lower to the ground, and they bring a sense of wonder and a more acute pair of eyes and ears.

Try new perspectives. At the Celery Farm, the easiest way to do this is to take two loops of the path, one in each direction. You'll see the same things, but from opposite vantage points. An analogy is the way that a nuthatch and a downy woodpecker operate. In search of food, the nuthatch works down the tree trunk, the woodpecker works up. Between them, they don't miss much.

Look behind you. To know where you're headed, it helps to see where you've been. You're less likely to get lost, and you may be surprised at what you missed — or what's gaining on you.

Stay put. Sometimes you'll observe and absorb the most by standing still. The observation platforms scattered around the lake (see map on page 33) are the places to watch for egrets, herons, cormorants, and various ducks.

You can do well by sitting on the bench by the butterfly garden or standing in the lowlands just to the south. Your patience will often be rewarded by the sight of an unusual insect — or a majestic red-tailed hawk.

In *Return of the Osprey*, David Gessner writes about the paradox of taking things slowly: "It leads to excitement that is often dazzling. What, after all, surprises and delights us? Speed.

Growth. Quantity. Vibrancy. Variety. These are the qualities that the natural world presents if we simply sit still and open our eyes."

Pay heed with your ears. Walking around the farm while listening to a Walkman is akin to wearing blinders. You may take years to begin to gain an expert's knowledge of calls, but even a casual walker can enjoy the insistent drumming of a woodpecker. Unless you're a parent of a toddler, you may be amazed that a creature so small can make a racket so large.

"One of the most secretive owls and a master of camouflage, the long-eared owl is not often seen. When perched against the trunk of a tree, its elongated shape, streaked body, and long ear tufts make it very much resemble a tree branch, not an owl."

— *Len Soucy,* New Jersey's Owls *(2000)*

Part of the art of seeing is picking out an object as unobtrusive as a Black-crowned Night Heron (inset) amid a sea of foliage.

Wood Duck   **Purple Gallinule**   **Green Heron**

The sound of the Northern Cardinal is as stunning and distinctive as his plumage, but perhaps the most exhilarating bird sound is not a call. It's the whoosh of wings as squadrons of migrating birds whisk overhead at dusk.

"We listen too much to the telephone and too little to nature," the conductor André Kostelanetz once observed. "The wind is one of my sounds. A lonely sound perhaps, but soothing.

"Everybody should have his own personal sounds to listen for — sounds that will make him exhilarated and alive, or quiet and calm." The Celery Farm has a wonderful inventory of sounds, if you'll take the time to listen.

Pay attention to the birds. The best way to spot a red-tailed hawk is to listen for the barking of crows. They will also sound the alarm if they see a fox or a mink on the prowl.

When a pheasant or duck or goose looks skyward, it's time to use your binoculars. A bird's-eye view is much sharper than a human's, and something is likely on wing.

Bring a magnifying glass. By seeing the little picture, you may get the big picture. You'll notice how the veins in your hand resemble the veins in a maple leaf and the tributaries of a river. A spider's web, a jewelweed pod ripe for popping, a fallen feather: With a magnifying glass, you can observe nature's brush strokes.

As Thoreau wrote in his journal more than 160 years ago: "Nature will bear the closest expression. She invites us to lay our eye level with her smallest leaf and take an insect view of its plane."

Along the way, you'll see more than nature's wonders. Instead of being lost in thought, you are freed from thought. Everyday problems — that unpaid bill, those hurt feelings, that missed opportunity — seem smaller. To lose oneself in nature can replenish the soul.

Syrphid Fly on Black-eyed Susan

Ruby-crowned Kinglet

Moving busily among

awakening spring leaves,

the kinglet

is here and gone

like a dream

— Brook Zelcer (2001)

Chapter 8

Out on a limb

"*Our birds are our men of genius. As in the literary world, there is a description of talent that must be discovered and pointed out by an observing few, before the great mass can understand it or even know its existence — so the sweetest songsters of the world are unknown to the mass of community, while many very ordinary performers whose talents are conspicuous are universally known and admired.*"

— *T. W. Higginson,* The Birds of Pasture and Forest *(1858)*

Young Green Herons nesting

Yellow Warbler with tree cricket

The next several pages provide an assortment of birds you might see over the course of a year if you visit the refuge often and look with sharp eyes. One of the first things a fledgling birder realizes is how difficult it is to identify so many kinds of birds — especially when the males and females may not look alike, the immature birds may not resemble the adults, and the plumage changes with the season.

This is a world of aviation wonder, from yellow-throats and yellow-rumps to red-bellied woodpeckers and rose-breasted grosbeaks. You needn't be able to identify them to enjoy their beauty and their songs, but with knowledge comes appreciation.

Red-winged Blackbird

Downy Woodpecker

Rose-breasted Grosbeak

Baltimore Oriole

Cedar Waxwing

"The silence of the cedar bird throws a mystery about him which neither his good looks nor his petty larcenies in cherry time can dispel."

— John Burroughs, Wake Robin *(1871)*

Yellow Warbler

Palm Warbler

Common Yellow-throat

Yellow-rumped Warbler

103

Red-bellied Woodpecker

"Sometimes a pair will take possession of a cavity already completed by some other woodpecker, and while such action may involve a moral question, it at least indicates a disposition to conserve physical effort which by many is today rated high among the vital resources of our country."

— *T. Gilbert Pearson*, Birds of America *(1917)*

House Finch

Goldfinch

Tree Swallow

Swamp Sparrow

American Robin

Eastern Kingbird

"This bird impresses me as a perfectly well-dressed and well-mannered person, who amid a very talkative society prefers to listen, and shows his character by action only."

— *T. W. Higginson,* The Life of Birds *(1862)*

"And what do I look for? Today, nothing more than the marsh, as unprepossessing as it is, with nothing much happening of an epochal nature. Just the marsh and me here today, and however trivial that may seem, in terms of my particular life lists, it is enough."

— *Jake Page*, Songs to Birds *(1993)*

Chapter 9

Memories

"Everybody needs beauty as well as bread, places to play

in and pray in, where nature may heal and give

strength to body and soul alike."

    — *John Muir,* The Yosemite *(1912)*

The Celery Farm contains a history beyond historical society archives, yellowed newspaper clippings, and the oral histories of those who worked there. This history resides in the collective memories of those who see it as just as much a sanctuary for them as it is for wildlife.

A man from Ho-Ho-Kus says that whenever he visits the Farm, he feels as though he is in church. A woman from another nearby town describes the Farm as her psychiatrist's couch. For others, memories of the refuge are bittersweet. One Allendale resident talks of coming to the Farm and meditating after his father's death — and proposing to his wife there.

Others come to read or meditate: a brand-new teacher reviewing lesson plans on a bench by the lake, a teenager reading a Bible on a viewing platform on a perfect June afternoon.

At dusk on the nightmarish day when terrorists hijacked airliners and destroyed the World Trade Center thirty miles away, several people gathered at the refuge's main platform to find an oasis of tranquility and mourn their losses and those of the nation.

Journalist Jennifer Kossak writes that when she sought solace there the next day, she sat alone with her thoughts, only to find herself "surrounded by a blizzard of warblers and vireos. The sight renewed my faith that, at the very least, the rhythm of nature had not been disturbed. Some things would remain constant, even now. . . . I have left seemingly unbearable sadness at the Celery Farm and have found my appreciation of life magnified a thousand-fold."

Even the cold of winter evokes strong memories. Writer Christopher DeVinck grew up nearby, and he has written about his childhood visits. In his book *Only the Heart Knows How to Find Them*, DeVinck writes that "Johnny and I spent many hours skating back and forth, chasing our sisters, polishing the ice with our mittens, and peering through the frozen water, looking nearly eye to eye with the large fish which passed under us like wandering spirits."

For journalist Charles McGrath, the Celery Farm was the inspiration for his article on pond hockey in the February 1997 issue of *Outside* magazine. He writes fondly of the spirited competition, then concludes on a more personal note: "My favorite memories are of the early mornings when I used to skate for an hour or so before school with my son. We'd get up when it was dark, and the sun would just be coming up, turning the marsh grass gray-gold, as my freezing fingers laced up his skates. We'd play a little one on one together or do little passing drills, and sometimes we'd just skate in parallel arcs and swirls — apart and yet together."

The memories differ, but in many ways they are the same: Each is highly personal, and each reflects a bond between humans or between humans and nature.

Wildlife needs a safe haven, a place away from the madding crowd, and so do humans. Everybody needs a Celery Farm.

Field near the old Bajor farm

"A pond is not much in and of itself, but add twilight, ducks and frogs, a great blue heron standing still, a mink circling the shore, and red-winged blackbirds singing from some shrubbery or swaying in the reeds, and then you have something special. These things are the pond. Take away one of these parts and the whole thing becomes diminished. Take away several parts and the setting becomes only a memory. As generations pass the memory fades, until nothing remains."

— *Bert C. Ebbers*, Nature's Places *(1992)*

Chapter 10

Preserving the refuge

"Our lives begin to end the day we become silent about things that matter."

— *Martin Luther King, Jr.*

For all its beauty, the true worth of the Celery Farm is as a functioning marsh. It provides precious habitat for birds and animals. It cleanses the water. It helps replenish the water supply during droughts. And it acts as an enormous sponge to ease flooding from heavy rains in an increasingly flood-prone region.

An extraordinary aspect of walking through the refuge is that it is unusual, and therein lies the tragedy. Decades ago, northeastern New Jersey brimmed with farms and wetlands and forests, and nearly every child hereabouts had places to explore. They could learn first-hand the wonders of nature, beginning with tadpoles, turtles, and toads. Those lessons are disappearing, and we all pay a price.

As the ancient Chinese Taoist philosopher Lao Tsu said: "In the end, we will conserve only what we love. We will love only what we understand. We will understand only what we are taught."

One way to ensure that those lessons continue is for us to celebrate the Celery Farm and other sanctuaries, and to bring our children and grandchildren. A few schools use the refuge as an opportunity for learning. It is one field trip that is literally a field trip.

Alas, some people have a compulsion to turn every acre of our dwindling natural open space into ball fields or recreational areas with picnic tables and lawns. For some, a park is not a park unless the thickets get thwacked and the ground gets leveled.

If this were to happen at the Celery Farm, the immediate losers would be all sorts of birds and animals who need untrammeled space to thrive. In the long run, we, too, would lose. This planet has been likened to a ship, with every kind of living creature representing a rivet that keeps the boat — our ecosystem — afloat. Lose too many rivets, and the boat sinks.

The Fyke Nature Association has several projects to help the Celery Farm's wildlife. It's tough to put up bird houses around the refuge because, as Marsh Warden Stiles Thomas has put it, "Bully, the English sparrow, takes over." But someone noticed tree swallows nesting in an old three-inch pipe jutting above Lake Appert. Fyke erected eight more pipes, and the little birds moved in. The swallows, who dine on mosquitoes and other bugs, are among the most environmentally friendly pesticides around.

Several years ago, Fyke erected seven nesting boxes in the lake's shallows. The wood ducks took to the waterside condos, and generations have hatched there.

Friends of the refuge have also reintroduced the ring-necked pheasant.

After a male — dubbed "Eyebrow" — was found in the phragmites in 1991, the group began to purchase and release hens. Over the years they've produced dozens of chicks.

What is the future of the Farm? Nothing lasts forever. Sooner or later, wetlands become uplands. Extensive development, decaying plants, and storm run-off create sediment that makes the water shallower, to the point where invasive plants take over and the marshes stop functioning.

Builders who seek to fill in marshes like to point out that they are merely accelerating nature's work. That's true, but many of the places where new marshes might occur have already been filled in or paved. Development puts a far greater strain on the few remaining wetlands, which must absorb more water from heavy rains and filter more pollutants.

To meet these threats to the Celery Farm and our other wetlands, we must act. Foremost, government must get serious about tackling stream and river pollution. Too many roadside pollutants — salt, motor oil, animal waste, cigarette butts, and other litter — get washed down storm sewers and into our creeks and brooks. Home owners rely on pesticides and fertilizer for "perfect" lawns, or drain chemical-laden swimming-pool water into the storm drains that empty into streams. Road salt has posed such a problem that the region's largest water company has alerted consumers with high blood pressure that their tap water has a high salinity.

Efforts are afoot to get local governments to switch from road salt to less-harmful ice melters, and to place warnings about misuse onto storm drains near waterways. If storm drains continue to collect plastic bottles, beverage cans, candy wrappers, and cigarette butts, it may be necessary to place nets on the handful of streams and brooks that feed the Celery Farm. At some point, dredging may be needed to ease years of silting.

Finally, there is the never-ending battle against all the invasive species that have taken root in the refuge: the wild rosebushes and knotweed that squeeze the paths each summer, the poison ivy trying to choke many of the trees, and the phragmites and loosestrife that dominate parts of the marsh. Humans may not win that war, but they must continue to keep these adversaries in check.

The other reason that the Celery Farm is invaluable is for the magnificent example it sets. The surest way to lose open space is to accept the argument that development is inevitable, that to fight it is to waste time, that a few do-gooders can't stop progress, and so on.

But democracy's great strength is that sometimes the backhoes meet obstacles they can't budge.

In Margaret Mead's words: "Never doubt that a small group of thoughtful, committed citizens can change the world. Indeed, it's the only thing that ever has."

Where the will to protect nature exists, so do the tools. Government programs such as New Jersey's Green Acres can help save land. Groups such as the New Jersey Conservation Foundation can provide the expertise. And places such as the Celery Farm are the proof.

When the world is too much with us, when somebody wants to subdivide the woods at the end of the block, when a condo is being crowbarred into that vacant lot around the corner — that's when a visit to the refuge reminds us that while humans need to conquer and build and pave, humans also need room to breathe.

The most invasive species known to man is man.

The Celery Farm serves as a reminder that with the help of a dedicated few, land that man has harnessed also can be set free.

A buck wading in Lake Appert

Index

Index

Bajor barn in autumn

Index

View from the Pirie Platform in autumn

Acknowledgments

Photography on pages 34, 83, 86, 99,100 (left) by Doug Goodell

Photography on pages 39, 53, 77, 91, 98,103 (upper left), 106, 117 by Patrick Sparkman

Photograph on page 93 by Mike Limatola

Photograph on page 6 (left) courtesy of Colleen FitzPatrick Tabatneck

Photographs on pages 61, 62, 64, 65, 68 courtesy of Allendale Historical Society

Photographs on pages 60, 64 courtesy of Mary Appert Schneider

Photograph on page 67 courtesy of Stiles Thomas

Lake Appert by moonlight

The authors wish to thank Stiles Thomas, Mike Limatola, Hugh Carola and the Fyke Nature Association, Michele Byers and the New Jersey Conservation Foundation, Deedee Burnside, Liz Houlton, Jim Brandenburg, Fred Ditmars, Joanne Hart, Dorothy Pennachio, Dianne DiBlasi, Mary Appert Schneider, David Epstein, Tom Oxnard, Kay Kidde, Michael Anastasio, Rob Fanning, the staff at the Lee Memorial Library, Robin Sparkman, the New Jersey Green Acres program, the borough of Allendale, Patricia Webb Wardell, Don Wallworth, Paul Shannon, Ed Benguiat, and everyone else who contributed so much to this book.

The authors also wish to thank all the volunteers who over the years have helped to make the Celery Farm a refuge for those who visit or live there, especially Lillian Thomas and John and Pat Brotherton, who have kept the butterfly garden in tip-top shape; Rob Pirie, who built two of the viewing platforms; the Allendale Newcomers Club, who purchased the materials for the Warden's Watch; Boy Scout Troop 59, who built the platform at the north end of the lake; Edward and Barbara Herbert, who donated three crucial acres; and Ken Appel, Bob Arata, Ken Buxton, Jim Kuehlke, Hans Sammer, and Jim Strauch, who have helped maintain the refuge for years.

Jerry Barrack uses Nikon equipment, especially N90 and F5 camera bodies. The lenses include an 18-35mm Sigma wide-angle, a Nikon 105mm macro, a Sigma 80-210 zoom, and most often a Nikon 600mm F4 telephoto lens with 1.4 and 2.0 extenders. Tripods are the Bogen 2021 and Gitzo 410. Films used were Fuji Velvia, Sensia, Provia, and Provia F pushed to 200 ASA. The only filters used were a circular polarizer and a graduated neutral density filter.

Jim Wright uses Bic and Papermate blue medium-point pens, Allied legal pads, and an iBook.

"That man is successful who has lived well, laughed often, and loved much,

who has gained the respect of the intelligent men and the love of children;

who has filled his niche and accomplished his task; who leaves the world

better than he found it, whether by an improved poppy, a perfect poem, or

a rescued soul; who never lacked appreciation of Earth's beauty or failed to

express it; who looked for the best in others and gave the best he had."

— Robert Louis Stevenson